DISNEY

The Enchanted Guide

Written by Julie Ferris

CONTENTS

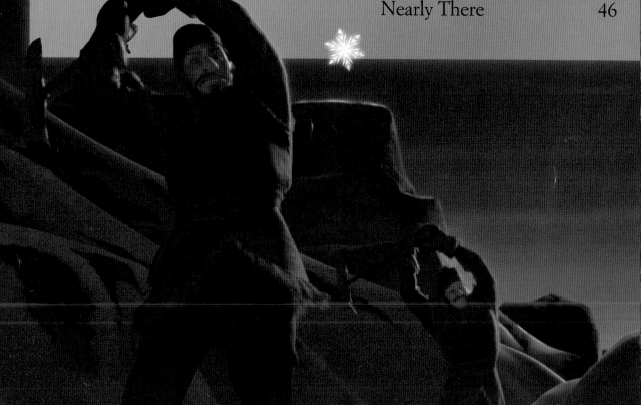

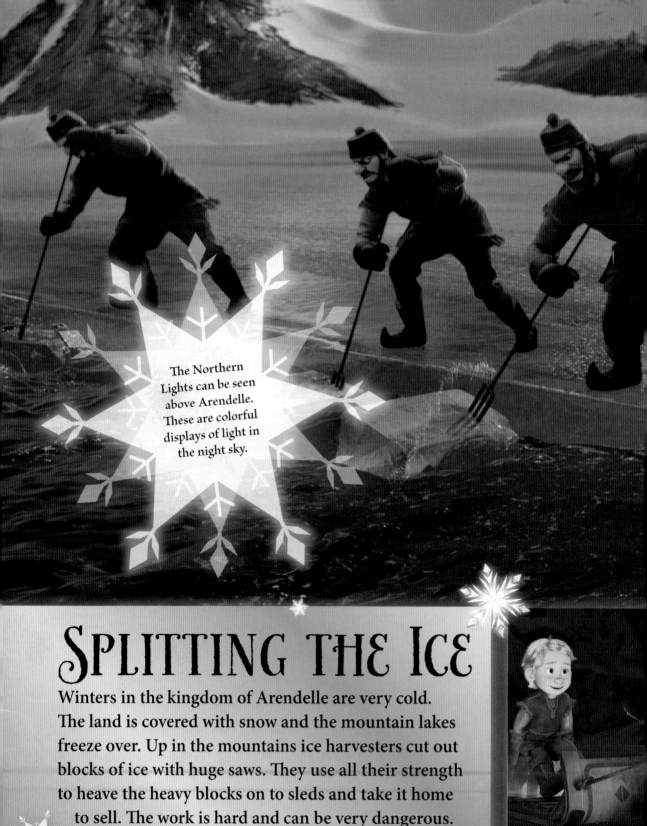

The Northern Lights can be seen above Arendelle. These are colorful displays of light in the night sky.

SPLITTING THE ICE

Winters in the kingdom of Arendelle are very cold. The land is covered with snow and the mountain lakes freeze over. Up in the mountains ice harvesters cut out blocks of ice with huge saws. They use all their strength to heave the heavy blocks on to sleds and take it home to sell. The work is hard and can be very dangerous.

Working together

A young mountain boy named Kristoff watches the strong men working. All he wants is to be an ice harvester when he grows up! He copies exactly what they do, helped by his trusted reindeer friend, Sven. They make a great team!

Slippery ice

Kristoff is only a small boy, but he is determined to keep up with the ice harvesters. He tries again and again to lift an ice block out of the water. It is slippery and heavy and keeps falling back in, but he will not give up.

The beautiful crocus is a well-known flower in Arendelle. It can be seen all over the castle and the kingdom.

Life in a castle

Arendelle's castle is a wonderful place to grow up. It has many grand rooms and the princesses love running through its long halls. From the castle tower, the girls can see the boats in Arendelle's beautiful harbor and the mountains in the distance.

PLAYTIME

At the heart of the kingdom of Arendelle is a magnificent castle, which is home to two young princesses named Elsa and Anna. Elsa, the elder sister, was born with magical ice powers. This means the girls can play wonderful games in the snow all year round!

"Do the magic! Do the magic!" Anna

Time to play

Late one night, Anna jumps onto Elsa's bed and wakes her up. She wants to play, but Elsa would much rather sleep. Refusing to give up, Anna asks Elsa if she wants to build a snowman with her. She knows that Elsa won't be able to resist!

Fun in the snow

The giggling princesses dash downstairs to the Great Hall. Elsa uses her magic to create sparkling snow and cover the floor in ice. A delighted Anna thinks that her sister's powers are truly amazing!

DISASTER STRIKES

Elsa uses her powers to create piles of snow for Anna to jump on. "Slow down!" Elsa cries, but Anna is too excited to listen and keeps jumping faster and faster. Just as Anna makes her biggest jump yet, Elsa slips on the ice. She tries to create a new pile of snow in time to catch her sister, but her aim misses and the magic strikes Anna's head instead. Anna falls to the ground, motionless, and a strand of her hair turns white.

> ## "Elsa! What have you done?"
> King Agnarr

"Mama! Papa!"

In a panic, Elsa calls for her parents. The king and queen rush to the Great Hall and are horrified to find Anna lying injured on the floor. The queen touches her and discovers that she is ice cold. Luckily, the king knows where they can go for help.

MEET THE KING AND QUEEN

King Agnarr and Queen Iduna are the rulers of Arendelle and the parents of Elsa and Anna. They are kind and strong leaders. Their kingdom is beautiful and prosperous and their people love them. The king and queen adore their daughters, but worry about the powers Elsa has been born with.

AGE: unknown

MOST LIKELY TO: do anything to protect their daughters

AMBITION: for Elsa to be a wise and kind queen when it is her turn to rule

FAVORITE THINGS: Anna and Elsa

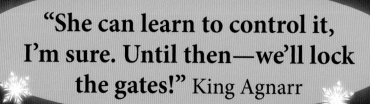

"She can learn to control it, I'm sure. Until then—we'll lock the gates!" King Agnarr

MEET GRAND PABBIE

Grand Pabbie is the leader of the trolls. He is both knowledgeable and kind, and he uses his strong magical powers to help those in need.

AGE: extremely ancient

MOST LIKELY TO: say something wise

FAVORITE THING: using his magic to heal and help others

HEALING POWERS

King Agnarr and Queen Iduna rush Anna to a faraway valley, home to the wise and ancient trolls. Grand Pabbie, the troll leader, uses his powers to make Anna better, and to wipe her memory so that she will not remember Elsa's magic. He warns Elsa that as her powers grow stronger, fear will be her enemy.

After Grand Pabbie heals Anna, her hair still has the white streak from when she was injured.

Disguised

When the king and queen and the two princesses arrive in the valley, there is no sign of the trolls. All they can see is a lot of big rocks lying around. But then the rocks begin to wobble and roll. They are trolls in disguise!

New family

Little Kristoff and Sven follow the icy trail Elsa leaves behind on her way to the valley. When they get there, they meet a troll named Bulda. Bulda is a motherly type. She thinks Kristoff and Sven are very cute, so she decides to adopt them.

> "Conceal it…"
> King Agnarr

> "…don't feel it."
> Elsa

HIDING THE MAGIC

The king orders the castle gates to be shut. The less contact Elsa has with people, the safer everyone will be. As time goes on, Elsa's magic gets more and more powerful, and it becomes harder for her to control it. To help her, the desperate king gives her some gloves to wear. As long as she keeps them on, she has a chance to hide her powers.

Elsa and Anna used to share a bedroom. However, after Anna's accident, Elsa moves to her own room.

Lockdown

After Anna's accident, only a few servants are allowed to remain in the castle. The gates are locked and the doors and windows shut. The people of Arendelle no longer see the princesses. Elsa's powers must be hidden from everyone.

Lonely Anna

Elsa shuts herself in her room and refuses to spend any time with Anna. She doesn't want to hurt her sister again. Anna can't understand why her sister won't talk to her. Without her best friend, she feels very lonely and confused.

A Tragic Loss

Many years pass and the castle doors remain shut.
One day, the king and queen set off on a voyage. Elsa
doesn't want them to leave—she is afraid to be alone with
her powers. The king reassures her that they will return
in only two weeks, but sadly he is wrong. They encounter
a terrible storm and their ship sinks. Elsa and Anna have
lost their parents and they are both truly devastated.

"What are we going to do?"
Anna

After Elsa loses her parents her grief shows itself through her magic. Her whole room fills with ice and snow.

In mourning

When news arrives that the king and queen's ship has sunk, the castle goes into mourning. Their portrait is covered by a black curtain as a sign of respect.

Anna's sorrow

Anna feels terribly alone. Elsa is the only family she has left in the world now, but when Anna tries to reach out to her, Elsa's door remains closed. Anna wants to be brave, but she struggles to cope with the awful tragedy all by herself.

OPEN AT LAST!

It is Coronation Day—the day that Elsa is to be crowned Queen of Arendelle. Anna can't believe it has finally arrived! For years, she has been shut inside the castle with no one to talk to. Now, the gates will open and crowds of people will come flooding in! However, Elsa does not share her sister's excitement. In fact, she has been dreading this day for many years.

MEET ANNA

A lively, playful princess, Anna dreams of parties and romance. She is sad and lonely in the locked castle and misses talking to her sister, Elsa.

AGE: 18

MOST LIKELY TO: not watch where she is going

AMBITION: to stop feeling lonely

Anna loves to sleep until late in the morning. A servant must wake her up so that she doesn't miss the coronation!

A dream of romance

Anna pretends to be the lady in the painting, and imagines what it will be like to meet real people. When the gates open, she will finally have the chance to make new friends, or maybe even fall in love!

Controlling the magic

Elsa is frightened of revealing her magic during the coronation ceremony. What will happen when she takes off her gloves? As she grows more nervous, she practices controlling her powers—and is horrified when she fails.

HANDSOME STRANGER

Anna runs through the streets of Arendelle, enjoying the
excitement of Coronation Day. As she reaches the harbor, she bumps
into a horse and almost ends up in the water! The horse's rider
introduces himself as Prince Hans of the Southern Isles. When he
hears that Anna is a princess, he bows gallantly and apologizes for
the accident—even though it wasn't his fault.

"I'd like to formally apologize for hitting the Princess of Arendelle with my horse." Hans

MEET PRINCE HANS OF THE SOUTHERN ISLES

As the youngest of 13 brothers, Prince Hans needs to marry into another royal family if he is to have any chance of ruling a kingdom. He may appear charming, but he is not as perfect as he seems.

AGE: 23
MOST LIKELY TO: hide the truth
AMBITION: to be a king
FAVORITE THING: himself

Lovestruck

Anna cannot stop staring at Prince Hans. She is not used to talking to handsome men, and finds herself blurting out that he is gorgeous. How very embarassing! Their conversation is cut short when Anna hears the bells for the coronation ceremony and rushes back to the castle.

Splash!

Hans feels so lucky to have met the Princess of Arendelle. As Anna hurries away, Hans is thrown into the water! However, he doesn't seem to mind getting wet. All he can do is gaze longingly after the beautiful princess. He hopes to meet her again soon.

"Queen Elsa of
Arendelle!"
Bishop

THE CORONATION

The coronation ceremony has begun! Elsa stands in the
cathedral, with everyone watching her. The moment she
has been dreading is nearly here. Soon she will have to
remove her gloves and pick up the orb and scepter.
Will she turn them to ice and reveal her secret?

MEET ELSA

Elsa is a very caring person, who feels the burden of her magic and of being queen. She is scared that people will discover her icy powers, or worse, that she could hurt someone. She desperately wants to do what's best for the people of Arendelle.

AGE: 21

MOST LIKELY TO: turn whatever she touches to ice

AMBITION: to avoid hurting anyone with her magic—especially her sister

FAVORITE THING: avoiding people

A shared moment

All of the guests are focused on Elsa, except for Hans. He only has eyes for Anna, and even the guest who has fallen asleep on his shoulder doesn't bother him! Hans and Anna give each other a little wave.

Just in time

Just as Elsa feared, her magic starts to freeze the orb and scepter! Is everyone going to see? Thankfully, she manages to return them to the cushion before anyone notices. She has made it through the ceremony, and her secret is still safe!

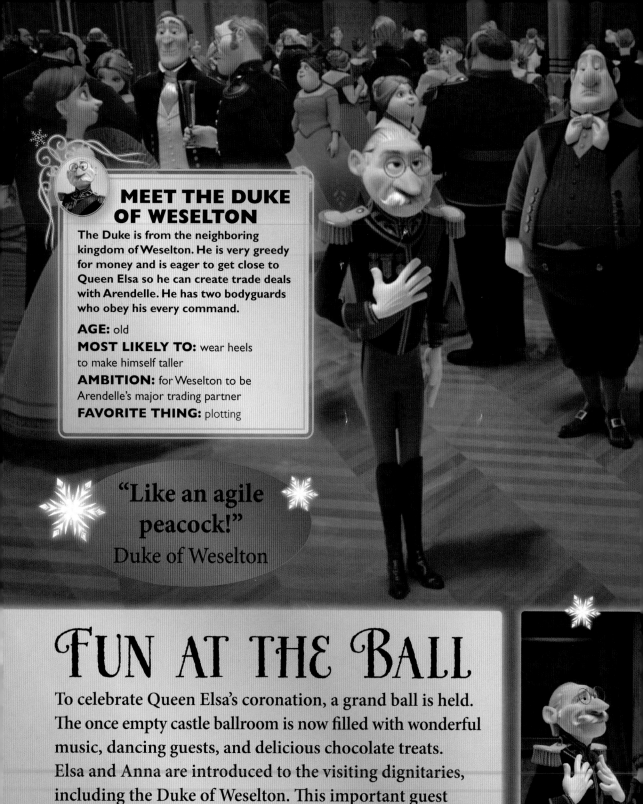

MEET THE DUKE OF WESELTON

The Duke is from the neighboring kingdom of Weselton. He is very greedy for money and is eager to get close to Queen Elsa so he can create trade deals with Arendelle. He has two bodyguards who obey his every command.

AGE: old

MOST LIKELY TO: wear heels to make himself taller

AMBITION: for Weselton to be Arendelle's major trading partner

FAVORITE THING: plotting

"Like an agile peacock!"
Duke of Weselton

FUN AT THE BALL

To celebrate Queen Elsa's coronation, a grand ball is held. The once empty castle ballroom is now filled with wonderful music, dancing guests, and delicious chocolate treats. Elsa and Anna are introduced to the visiting dignitaries, including the Duke of Weselton. This important guest makes a big impression with his unusual dance moves!

Grand introduction

The servant who introduces the Duke of Weselton mistakenly calls him the "Duke of Weaseltown"! The Duke is very cross and quickly corrects the servant. The Duke is eager to sound important, so he reminds Elsa that Weselton is Arendelle's closest trade partner.

Showing off

The Duke asks Elsa to dance, but she suggests that Anna would make a better partner. Poor Anna is flung across the dance floor as the Duke shows off his skills! Unfortunately, his crazy dancing also causes his wig to lose its place, revealing his bald head!

23

Anna Falls in Love

Anna's evening suddenly gets much better when Hans arrives at the ball. Anna had wondered if she might meet the man of her dreams today, and here he is! The couple spends the evening talking and laughing, and they cannot take their eyes off each other. When Hans asks Anna to marry him, she doesn't hesitate. She says yes!

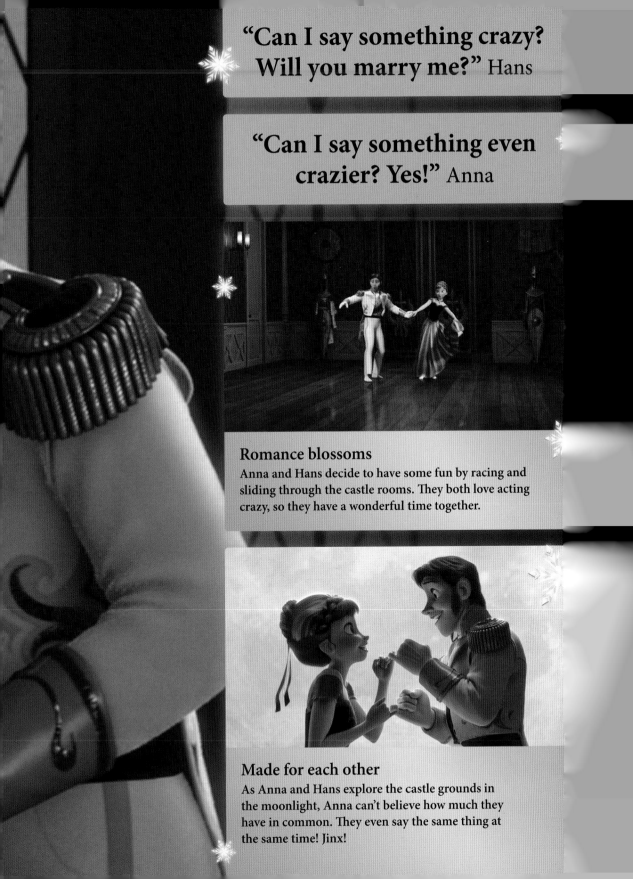

> **"Can I say something crazy? Will you marry me?"** Hans

> **"Can I say something even crazier? Yes!"** Anna

Romance blossoms

Anna and Hans decide to have some fun by racing and sliding through the castle rooms. They both love acting crazy, so they have a wonderful time together.

Made for each other

As Anna and Hans explore the castle grounds in the moonlight, Anna can't believe how much they have in common. They even say the same thing at the same time! Jinx!

ELSA'S POWERS REVEALED

Anna excitedly asks Elsa to bless her marriage to Hans. But Elsa insists that Anna can't marry a man she has just met! As the sisters' argument gets more heated, Elsa loses her cool and blasts spikes of ice across the ballroom. The secret she has tried so hard to hide is out at last!

If Anna had not snatched Elsa's glove, Elsa's powers might have remained hidden forever.

"Why do you shut the world out?"
Anna

Sisters divided
Anna desperately tries to make Elsa understand that she can't live such a lonely life anymore. She is shocked and hurt when Elsa tells her that maybe she should leave Arendelle.

The glove is off
As the sisters argue, Anna snatches at Elsa's hand and pulls her glove off. Without its protection, Elsa's magic can't be hidden. Anna had no idea that Elsa was hiding such a big secret—until now!

27

FEAR COMES TO ARENDELLE

Elsa is horrified that her secret has been uncovered. She runs out into the castle courtyard, only to find that all the people of Arendelle are waiting there to greet their new queen! Stumbling through the crowds, her hand touches the edge of the fountain. To everyone's shock, it freezes, its flow suspended in midair.

"Monster!"
Duke of Weselton

Frozen fountain
When the Duke of Weselton calls for Elsa to be stopped, Elsa begs him to stay away from her. Another bolt of magic accidentally shoots from her hand, and the Duke slips on the icy ground.

Frozen fjord
Desperate to get away from everyone, Elsa reaches the edge of the fjord. As her foot touches the water, it turns to ice. She realizes that she can run across it, the water freezing with each step.

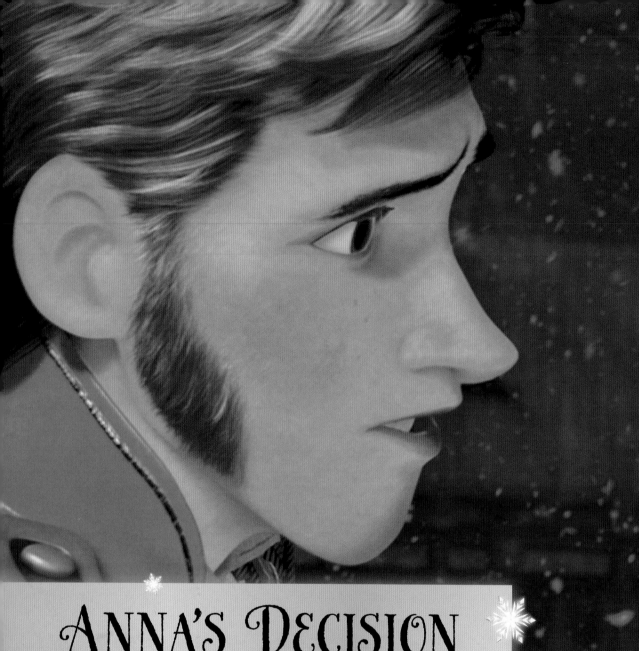

ANNA'S DECISION

Anna is very worried about Elsa. She decides that it is her
responsibility to find her sister and bring her back home.
Before she leaves, Anna places Prince Hans in charge of
Arendelle. She mounts her horse and gallops away from
the castle. It is midsummer, but snow is falling…

"She's my sister. She would never hurt me."

Anna

Defending Elsa

The Duke of Weselton demands to know if Anna also has powers. Anna assures him that she is completely ordinary. She insists that Elsa means no harm, but the Duke does not believe her.

THE ICE PALACE

As Elsa heads towards the North Mountain, she is finally free to stop hiding and be herself. She is excited to see what her magic can really do now that she no longer has to worry about hurting anyone else. She creates a beautiful, glistening ice palace—the perfect home for a queen with ice powers.

Elsa's ice palace is built around the hexagonal shape of a snowflake.

Snow magic

As she makes her way up the mountain, Elsa uses her magic to make shimmering snow flurries. She even creates a cute snowman just like the one she made for Anna when they were children.

Elsa's makeover

It's time for a new look! Elsa uses her powers to turn her heavy royal robes into a beautiful, flowing gown, which sparkles with snowflakes. Her crown is thrown away and her tight hair bun is let down into a loose braid.

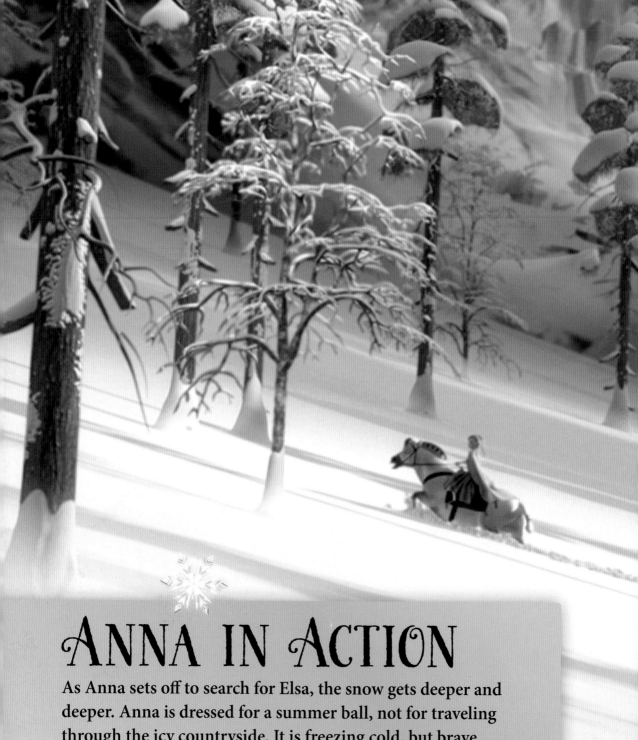

ANNA IN ACTION

As Anna sets off to search for Elsa, the snow gets deeper and deeper. Anna is dressed for a summer ball, not for traveling through the icy countryside. It is freezing cold, but brave Anna is determined to keep going. She has to find her sister!

"It had to be snow! She couldn't have tropical magic!" Anna

Going on alone

As Anna climbs through the snowy hills on horseback, a huge pile of snow falls on top of her. The frightened horse throws Anna to the ground and bolts. Now she is completely alone, but she doesn't give up. Nothing will stop her from bringing Elsa home.

Shelter at last!

Freezing cold, soaking wet, and completely fed up, Anna stumbles through the woods. She has no idea which direction to go in. Suddenly, she spots smoke in the distance. It is coming from the chimney of a cozy-looking wooden cabin. Anna rushes toward it, desperate to get warm.

STORE MEETING

The wooden cabin that Anna stumbles across is Wandering Oaken's Trading Post. The winter weather has taken Oaken the storekeeper by surprise. Usually he would be selling lots of summer goods at this time of year. But who wants to buy swimsuits in this cold weather? Anna finds a warm outfit and boots to buy for her snowy journey. As she approaches the counter, an ice-covered Kristoff stomps into the store.

MEET OAKEN

Oaken is usually very friendly, but he can sometimes have quite a temper. He is proud of his store and is a great salesman. He is always thinking of new ways to entice customers and increase his sales.

MOST LIKELY TO: wear a brightly-colored sweater

AMBITION: to predict the supply and demand issues of Arendelle

FAVORITE THING: offering customers a visit to the store's sauna

"Big summer blowout!" Oaken

Thrown out!

Kristoff thinks that Oaken's prices are too high, and isn't afraid to call him a crook. Oaken swiftly loses his cool with his rude customer and throws Kristoff out into the snow.

Sven can't speak, but Kristoff understands what his looks and grunts mean, and he can translate them.

LOOKING FOR A GUIDE

Anna needs help finding her sister, and she thinks that Kristoff would be an excellent guide. She finds Kristoff and asks him to take her up the North Mountain. At first he refuses, but when Anna says that she knows how to stop the winter, he agrees to take her.

MEET SVEN

Kristoff found Sven when he was just a calf. They have grown up together and are best friends. Sven helps Kristoff with his ice business by pulling the sled loaded with blocks of ice.

AGE: 21

MOST LIKELY TO: do (almost) anything for carrots

AMBITION: to make sure Kristoff is happy

FAVORITE THING: carrots

A song for Sven

Before Anna arrives, Kristoff plays his lute and sings a soothing bedtime song. He enjoys pretending that Sven is singing the song along with him. It's quite an unusual duet!

Anna's gift

Anna has bought Kristoff the rope and ax he needed from Oaken's Trading Post. She even treats Sven to the carrots he had been hoping for. Anna hopes this might persuade Kristoff to agree to help her.

"Get ready to
jump, Sven!"
Anna

DANGER!

As Kristoff, Anna, and Sven race through the forest,
they hear terrifying snarls and are horrified to see many
pairs of eyes peering at them through the darkness.
They are being chased by a pack of wolves! Sven gallops
away as fast as he can, but it is not fast enough. A wolf
pulls Kristoff off the sled, but quick-thinking Anna
frightens it off with a burning blanket.

MEET KRISTOFF

Kristoff grew up in the forests of Arendelle with his best friend, Sven. He was raised by the trolls and considers them his family. He works as an ice harvester, but the eternal winter means there is little demand for ice. He is more cautious than Anna, but he admires her sense of adventure.

MOST LIKELY TO: help the people he loves

AMBITION: to have a successful ice harvesting business

FAVORITE THING: his sled

A daring leap

As the ferocious wolves chase the trio through the trees, the sled approaches a huge ravine. Kristoff throws Anna onto Sven's back and the two leap across to the other side. Kristoff jumps after them but almost doesn't make it! Fortunately, Anna and Sven manage to pull him to safety.

Smashed sled

Kristoff, Anna, and Sven are safe from the wolves, but Kristoff's sled lies broken in pieces at the bottom of the ravine. Anna promises to replace it, but Kristoff begins to wish that he had never started on this journey with her.

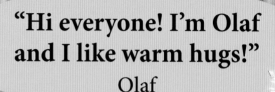

MEET OLAF

Olaf may be made of snow, but he has a very warm heart. He is a loyal friend and can be very wise, especially in matters of love.

AGE: one day old

MOST LIKELY TO: look on the bright side of life

AMBITION: to go on a summer beach vacation

FAVORITE THING: warm hugs

FRIENDLY SNOWMAN

As Anna, Kristoff, and Sven travel through the snowy forest, they are startled to meet a walking, talking snowman! Anna screams in shock and accidentally kicks his head off, but the cheerful snowman doesn't seem to mind. He tells them that his name is Olaf and explains that Elsa built him. Anna suddenly remembers playing with him and Elsa many years ago, back in happier times. It is soon clear from talking to Olaf that he is not scary at all.

Olaf is confused at first, and thinks that Kristoff and his reindeer friend are both called Sven!

Carrot nose

Olaf is missing an important snowman feature—a nose! Anna takes one of Sven's carrots and pushes it into Olaf's face. At first she pushes too hard and the carrot pokes through the other side of his head! She rearranges it until Olaf's nose looks perfect.

In summer!

Anna and Kristoff tell Olaf that they are trying to find Elsa so that summer can return to Arendelle. Olaf is eager to help them, as he has never experienced summer and imagines he would love it. He has no idea what actually happens to snow in the heat!

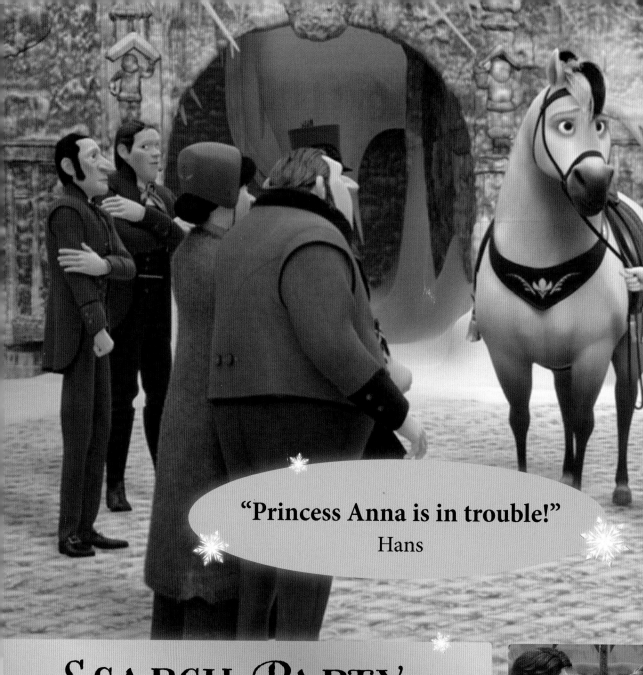

"**Princess Anna is in trouble!**"
Hans

SEARCH PARTY

Back at the castle, Anna's horse gallops into the courtyard without her. Hans knows that Anna must be in trouble. He asks for volunteers to go with him to find her and bring her safely back to Arendelle.

Taking charge

The townspeople are struggling to cope with the unexpected winter. Hans gives out warm cloaks and tells the people that there is hot food and shelter for them in the castle. He is enjoying being in charge.

Sneaky plan

The Duke of Weselton volunteers his two bodyguards to join the search party. He makes sure the men know that if they find Elsa they are to destroy her. That should put an end to this winter!

NEARLY THERE

Kristoff climbs Elsa's ice staircase in a daze. All his life, he has worked at harvesting ice blocks, but he never knew ice could be made to look like this. It's so beautiful he thinks he might cry! Meanwhile, Anna is already at the top of the stairs, preparing to face her sister in her ice palace.

Will she be allowed in, or will Elsa send her away?

"Nobody wants to be alone!" Anna

It's Olaf who finds the ice staircase—Anna and Kristoff are too busy arguing to notice it!

Tricky climb

Before the group notices the ice staircase, Anna tries to climb straight up the side of the mountain. She is determined to reach Elsa, and ignores Kristoff when he tells her to stop. However, she is pretty relieved when she realizes that she can take the stairs instead!

Slippery Sven

Poor Sven! He tries his best to climb the staircase, but his hooves just slide on the slippery surface. It's obvious that reindeer aren't built to climb icy stairs. Kristoff helps him back down and tells him to wait at the bottom. Sven doesn't have much choice!

"I'm just trying to protect you!"
Elsa

THE DOOR OPENS

Anna has found Elsa at last! As she enters Elsa's beautiful ice palace, she is sure that she can persuade her sister to return to Arendelle and bring back summer. Anna doesn't remember that Elsa accidentally hurt her when they were children, but Elsa has not forgotten. She is terrified of hurting Anna again.

Hesitation

Anna is scared to knock on the door of
the palace. When she was a little girl, she
knocked and knocked on Elsa's bedroom
door and Elsa never let her in. Is the same

Out in the cold

Elsa's ice palace is more beautiful than anything
Kristoff has ever dreamed of. He would love to
go inside and explore. However, Anna tells
him he has to stay outside so she can talk

49

ELSA'S DESPAIR

Elsa is shocked to hear that her powers have cast an eternal winter on Arendelle. She had been so sure that by hiding away on the mountain, she was keeping Arendelle safe. Anna thinks that all Elsa has to do is unfreeze everything, but it's not that simple—Elsa doesn't know how! Will she ever be free from the danger that comes with her magic?

"You kind of set off an eternal winter… everywhere." Anna

Elsa and Olaf

Elsa created a snowman on her way up the mountain, but she had no idea that he had come to life! Seeing Olaf walk into her ice palace gives her a big surprise. It makes her see that her magic is far more powerful than she ever imagined.

Losing control

Elsa begs Anna to leave, but Anna refuses to return to Arendelle without her sister. Elsa's anger and frustration cause her to lose control of her magic. It bursts out of her and strikes Anna in the heart! A shocked Anna stumbles and falls to the ground.

Marshmallow is so big and strong that he can pick up trees and throw them as if they were matchsticks.

Get Out!

Elsa is horrified to have hurt Anna with her powers a second time, and is desperate to make her leave before things get worse. She creates a huge, terrifying snowman, who throws Anna out of the palace along with Kristoff and Olaf. When Anna angrily throws a snowball at him, he starts to chase them down the mountain!

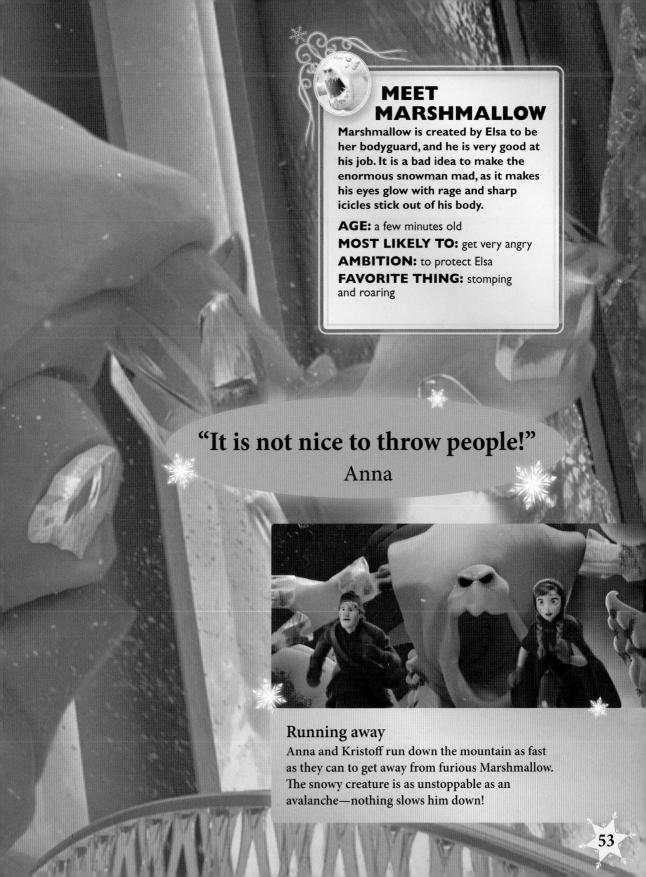

MEET MARSHMALLOW

Marshmallow is created by Elsa to be her bodyguard, and he is very good at his job. It is a bad idea to make the enormous snowman mad, as it makes his eyes glow with rage and sharp icicles stick out of his body.

AGE: a few minutes old
MOST LIKELY TO: get very angry
AMBITION: to protect Elsa
FAVORITE THING: stomping and roaring

"It is not nice to throw people!"
Anna

Running away

Anna and Kristoff run down the mountain as fast as they can to get away from furious Marshmallow. The snowy creature is as unstoppable as an avalanche—nothing slows him down!

Olaf is excited when he first sees Marshmallow. He doesn't realize that his fellow snowman isn't as friendly as he is!

A Great Escape

Anna and Kristoff run, slip, and slide down the mountain, desperate to get away from Marshmallow. They think they have escaped by lowering themselves on a rope over a cliff. Suddenly Marshmallow grabs the rope and starts to pull them back up again! With no other way out, Anna cuts the rope, and they plunge down onto soft, powdery snow.

"Don't come back!"
Marshmallow

Olaf tries to help
Brave Olaf tries to stop Marshmallow from chasing his friends by clinging on to the monster's leg. Unfortunately, Olaf's efforts are wasted and Marshmallow easily kicks Olaf off the cliff.

Anna in trouble
Kristoff notices that Anna's hair is turning white. Being struck by Elsa's powers is starting to affect her. Anna begins to worry, but Kristoff has an idea! He knows where they can go for help.

"Meet my family!"
Kristoff

The valley is the only place in Arendelle that isn't covered with Elsa's magical snow.

TROLL VALLEY

When Kristoff was a little boy, he watched Grand Pabbie, the leader of the trolls, heal Anna. Now that Anna has been hurt again by Elsa's magic, Kristoff knows that he must take her back to Troll Valley as quickly as possible. He's sure that Grand Pabbie will be able to help again. However, he doesn't know that a frozen heart cannot be healed as easily as a frozen head.

Warming up

Anna's injury is making her colder and colder. Kristoff wants to help, but what can he do? Then he notices a hot steam vent shooting up from the ground and eagerly leads Anna over to it. A grateful Anna warms herself a little before they continue.

Puzzled

When the trolls are resting they look like rocks lying on the ground. When Kristoff starts talking to these rocks, Anna and Olaf think he has gone crazy! Olaf tells Anna that he'll distract Kristoff so that she can run away.

A Troll Wedding

The trolls are thrilled to see their beloved Kristoff, and when they realize he has brought a girl with him they are doubly excited! Kristoff and Anna try to explain that they are not a couple, but the trolls simply won't listen. In their eyes, Kristoff and Anna are clearly perfect for each other, and so a troll wedding must take place. But then Anna collapses, overcome by the ice in her heart. She needs Grand Pabbie's help, urgently!

MEET BULDA

Bulda is a warm and motherly troll who adopted Kristoff and Sven when they were little. Bulda is very caring, but tends to interfere in Kristoff's life and is sure she knows what is best for him.

AGE: it is rude to ask a lady troll her age!

MOST LIKELY TO: meddle in affairs of the heart

AMBITION: to see Kristoff married

FAVORITE THINGS: Kristoff and Sven

The trolls wear beautiful, glowing crystals around their necks. They shine brightly in dazzling red, blue, green, and pink!

"He's brought a girl!"
Bulda

A wife for Kristoff!
The protective trolls only want the best for their Kristoff, even though they know he's far from perfect. As soon as Bulda meets Anna she doesn't hesitate to take a closer look! Bulda is pleased with Anna's bright eyes and strong teeth—she will do nicely!

Act of true love
Grand Pabbie tells Anna that her life is in danger! Only an act of true love can save her—otherwise she will turn to solid ice. "A true love's kiss, perhaps?" suggests Bulda. Kristoff realizes he must get Anna to Hans as soon as possible, so that Hans can kiss her and save her life.

BATTLE AT THE ICE PALACE

Elsa thinks the danger is over now that Anna and Kristoff are off the mountain—but she couldn't be more wrong. Hans and his search party have arrived at the ice palace, with the Duke of Weselton's murderous bodyguards among them. They sneak inside, determined to destroy Elsa! Little do the Duke's men know, they stand no chance against Elsa's strong powers.

At first, the search party doesn't notice Marshmallow. He looks like a huge mound of snow!

"Queen Elsa! Don't be the monster they fear you are!" Hans

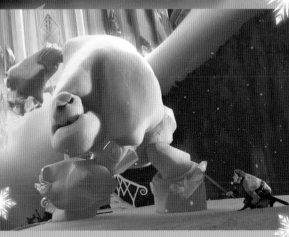

Defeating Marshmallow

Even though Marshmallow is huge and terrifying, Hans fearlessly attacks him and cuts off his leg. Marshmallow loses his balance and tumbles off the edge of the mountain.

Wise words from Hans

Hans dashes into the palace, just in time to stop Elsa from harming the Duke of Weselton's bodyguards. Hans makes Elsa understand that if she does not spare their lives, she will only make people even more afraid of her powers.

Captured

Elsa wakes up in a prison cell in Arendelle,
with no memory of how she got there. Iron gloves
cover her hands to stop her from using her magic
and escaping. She is shocked when Hans enters
the cell and tells her that she has been locked
up for her own protection.

"What have I done?"
Elsa

Icy scene
When Elsa looks through her cell window she is devastated to see for herself the deep winter her magic has caused. Hans begs her to bring back summer, but she explains that she can't—she simply doesn't know how!

Strong magic
Hans believes that the iron gloves will prevent Elsa from being able to use her magic. But as she gets more and more upset, the gloves begin to freeze. Elsa's magic is more powerful than Hans could ever imagine.

Anna Returns

Sven gallops towards Arendelle, while Kristoff cradles Anna in his arms. As Anna grows weaker, Kristoff urges Sven to go even faster. He knows he has to get her to Hans, who can give her the true love's kiss that will save her life! At the castle gates, the servants are relieved to see Anna but they are alarmed at how sick she is.

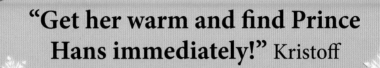

"Get her warm and find Prince Hans immediately!" Kristoff

Can't stay quiet

As Olaf whizzes down the mountain alongside Sven, Kristoff warns the snowman to keep out of sight once he reaches Arendelle. But friendly Olaf can't resist saying hello to a townswoman, who screams in shock!

Kristoff's farewell

Sven watches sadly as Kristoff leaves Anna behind at the castle. Kristoff thinks that delivering Anna to her true love is the right thing to do—even if it breaks his heart. Now he has to walk away from Anna forever.

> "Oh, Anna. If only there was someone out there who loved you." Hans

A WICKED PRINCE

As soon as Anna sees Hans, she begs him to kiss her. Anna explains that Elsa froze her heart and only an act of true love can save her now. Hans cruelly tells Anna that he won't kiss her, and that he never loved her at all! He knows that if Anna dies and Elsa gets the blame, then he can become the ruler of Arendelle. Evil Hans locks Anna in the library and tells everyone that she is dead—killed by Queen Elsa!

Hans thinks that his plan has worked perfectly. The arrogant prince is sure that nothing will stop him now.

Betrayal!
The cold-hearted Hans puts out the fire in the library. This makes the room freezing cold. Now Anna has to struggle even harder to stay alive. Unless someone comes to help her, she has no hope of surviving!

Evil Hans
Hans tells Anna that he is going to kill Elsa and bring back summer. He says everyone will think of him as a hero because he has saved Arendelle from destruction! Weak and cold, Anna is powerless to stop him.

ELSA FLEES

As the new ruler of Arendelle, Hans charges Elsa with treason and sentences her to death. Elsa is still locked in her cell and tries desperately to free herself. Her power is growing stronger with every minute. When Hans and the guards burst into the dungeon, all they see is an empty room. Hans is furious to find a gaping hole in the wall and the gloves lying shattered on the floor. Elsa has escaped!

> ## "With a heavy heart, I charge Queen Elsa of Arendelle with treason."
> Hans

A shameless lie

Hans tells the dignitaries that he and Anna said their marriage vows and that Anna died shortly afterwards. The dignitaries confirm that this means Hans is now the rightful ruler of Arendelle.

Storm in Arendelle

As Elsa gets more upset, she has less and less control over her icy powers. Without meaning to, she unleashes a devastating blizzard over Arendelle. The freezing wind howls, ice creeps through the castle walls, and the snow falls so thickly that it is impossible to see.

TURNING BACK

Kristoff trudges slowly back up the mountain. He is devastated to have to leave Anna behind, but he believes that she belongs with her true love, Hans. Sven tries to persuade Kristoff to turn back, but Kristoff refuses. Suddenly, he feels a strong gust of wind, and turns around to see a terrible snowstorm swirling above the castle. Anna is in danger!

> "No, Sven, we're not going back! She's with her true love."
> Kristoff

Sven's wisdom

Sven may not be able to speak, but he makes it very clear to Kristoff that they should return to Arendelle. Usually, Sven does what Kristoff tells him to, but not this time! He tries his very best to persuade Kristoff to go and fight for Anna.

Anna in danger

As soon as Kristoff sees the storm surrounding the castle, he knows he has made a terrible mistake in leaving Anna. He must get back to her as soon as possible! As the storm grows stronger, Kristoff and Sven race down the mountain at top speed.

71

Olaf is very resourceful. He uses his carrot nose to pick the lock of the library door.

OLAF TO THE RESCUE

Just as Anna is giving up hope, Olaf appears! He immediately lights a fire and pulls his freezing friend close to the heat. Anna tells Olaf that she was wrong about Hans and that she doesn't know what love is after all. He explains that love is putting other people's needs first, like when Kristoff brought Anna to Hans. Suddenly Anna realizes what Olaf knew all along—Kristoff is the one who loves her!

"So this is heat!" Olaf loves the feeling of heat. But as his wooden hand catches fire and then his face begins to melt, he figures out that heat holds great danger for a snowman.

"Some people are worth melting for."
Olaf

Kristoff returns

A gust of icy wind flings open the window. Olaf goes to close it, but wait—there's something in the distance! Olaf uses an icicle as a telescope so he can get a closer look. It's Kristoff, coming to rescue Anna!

Snowman to snowball

When Olaf reaches the ground, he finds that his roll down the roof has turned him into a giant snowball! He manages to shake off the extra snow, but the strong wind soon causes him to blow away. Anna must carry on alone.

LAST CHANCE

There is no time to lose! Olaf must get Anna to Kristoff before she turns to ice! He breaks a window leading out on to the snow-covered castle roofs and they both slide down to the ground. Although they land safely, they still can't find a way to reach Kristoff. The swirling snow means they cannot see where he is, and the howling wind makes it almost impossible to stand up.

"Keep going, Anna!"
Olaf

Dangerous path

The blizzard is becoming stronger and stronger, but Kristoff and Sven don't slow down. They are determined to rescue Anna. A ship, broken up by the ice, falls sideways and nearly crashes on top of them, but they manage to gallop past it just in time!

Icy hands

Anna stumbles around on the ice, desperately calling for Kristoff. Her weak voice is completely lost in the raging storm. To her horror, when she glances down at her hands she sees that they are turning to ice!

Anna's Sacrifice

Hans finds Elsa on the frozen fjord, and tells her that her magic has killed Anna! Elsa is so overcome at hearing this news, she falls to the ground and the blizzard stops. Anna and Kristoff can finally see each other. But as Kristoff runs towards her, Anna notices that Hans is standing over Elsa with his sword raised. In a courageous act of self-sacrifice, Anna turns away from Kristoff and uses all her remaining strength to shield Elsa from Hans' sword.

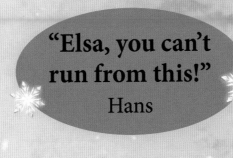

> ## "Elsa, you can't run from this!"
> Hans

Elsa is so shocked when she hears about her sister's death that her magic causes the snowstorm to instantly turn still and eerily silent.

Shattered

As Hans' sword comes down, it strikes Anna's raised hand, just as she turns to solid ice. The sword blade shatters and the force of the magic throws Hans backward. His wicked plan is foiled!

Last breath

A final breath leaves Anna's mouth as her body turns to ice. She has saved Elsa's life, but in doing so she has given up the chance to be saved by a true love's kiss from Kristoff.

LOVE WILL THAW

Broken-hearted Elsa's worst fear has come true—she has lost Anna because of her icy powers. She wraps her arms round her sister's frozen body and weeps. Then Olaf notices Anna slowly starting to thaw, and the life returning to her body! Anna's sacrifice for Elsa was the act of true love that thawed her heart!

> "An act of true love will thaw a frozen heart."
>
> Olaf

The end of winter
Elsa is so happy that Anna is alive! She finally knows how to control her powers—with love. The people of Arendelle watch in awe as she makes the snow disappear, the sun come out, and the frozen fjord turn to water once again.

A flurry for Olaf
The end of winter is good news for everyone except Olaf. He now knows that snowmen don't last very long in the sunshine! As the weather grows warm, his body begins to melt. Elsa quickly comes to the rescue, making him his own snow flurry to keep him cool.

GOOD RIDDANCE!

Now that summer has returned, there is just one last thing for Anna and Elsa to take care of. They order Hans to be thrown into the cramped cell of a ship, which will return him to the Southern Isles. The devious prince's 12 brothers are sure to deal with his bad behavior on his return!

Anna's revenge

Hans is shocked when he sees that Anna is alive and well. He thought her heart had been frozen. Anna makes it completely clear how she feels about Hans. She punches him and he falls backward into the fjord!

"The only frozen heart around here is yours!"
Anna

Farewell to the Duke
The Duke of Weselton is soon sent away, too. Queen Elsa has ordered that there be no further trade between Arendelle and Weselton. A faithful palace servant enjoys delivering the message! Now the Duke's dreams of getting his hands on Arendelle's riches are over.

ROMANCE BLOSSOMS

Anna has a surprise for Kristoff—it's a new sled for his ice business, to replace the one that was destroyed during their adventures. Kristoff is completely thrilled, but he doesn't go and sit in the sled straight away. Instead, he swings Anna round and round with joy. At long last, it's time for the two of them to admit how much they care for each other!

Kristoff's new job
Kristoff's new sled is the latest model. It even has a cup holder! Elsa has appointed Kristoff the Official Arendelle Ice Master and Deliverer.

Sven hasn't been forgotten by Anna. She gives him a medal to wear around his neck.

"I could kiss you!"
Kristoff

TIME TO CELEBRATE!

Elsa has learned that she can control her magic with the power of love. She thinks of the perfect way to celebrate—a beautiful ice rink in the castle courtyard. The people of Arendelle look on in delight as the cobbles freeze over and the fountains are transformed into ice sculptures. Elsa also uses her powers to give Anna a pair of skates so she can join in the fun.

"I like the open gates." Anna

"We are never closing them again!" Elsa

Anna and Elsa skate around with Olaf, just as they did in the Great Hall when they were children.

Atchoo!

At long last, Olaf is able to enjoy summer, just as he has always dreamed. Disaster nearly strikes when he sneezes and his nose flies into Sven's mouth! Luckily, Sven doesn't give in to the temptation to eat it— he returns it to his new friend.

"I just want it to be perfect."
Elsa

Everything for Anna's party is decorated with sunflowers—from the cake to the balloons!

ANXIOUS ELSA

Many harmonious months pass by in Arendelle, until a very exciting day arrives—Anna's birthday! Now that the sisters are close again, Elsa is determined to make it truly special, with presents and a surprise party.

When the big day finally arrives, she is anxious to make sure that every little detail is absolutely perfect.

Party planners

Kristoff and Sven are hard at work creating a large birthday banner for the courtyard. It might not look the way Elsa would have liked, but they are pretty pleased with their efforts! When Elsa sets off to celebrate with Anna, she leaves them to finish the decorating.

Excited Olaf

Anna's four-tiered ice cream cake is just too tempting for Olaf to resist. He sneakily swipes some delicious frosting— but Elsa catches him in the act. The guilty snowman sticks his half-eaten frosting back on the cake.

BIRTHDAY SURPRISES

As soon as the morning bell chimes, Elsa rushes to Anna's bedroom and wakes up the sleepy birthday girl. She gives Anna a beautiful new dress to wear, using her magic to give it extra sparkle. As Anna finishes getting ready, Elsa sneezes. Anna wonders if Elsa has caught a cold, but Elsa insists that she is perfectly fine.

"We need to get our birthday chills—I mean thrills." Elsa

Treasure hunt

Elsa tells Anna to follow a red string, which takes the sisters on a treasure hunt across the kingdom. It leads Anna to many wonderful presents, including sunflowers, sandwiches, and a cuckoo clock!

Feeling weak

To Elsa's dismay, her cold grows worse as the day goes on. She tries her best to keep celebrating with her sister, but she can't stop sneezing and shivering. Anna eventually convinces her that they have done quite enough celebrating for one day, and that they should return to the castle.

89

CHAOS IN THE COURTYARD

Every time Elsa sneezes, her icy magic causes tiny, mischievous snowmen to appear. When the little snowmen spot Anna's cake, they waste no time trying to take it for themselves! Kristoff, Sven, and Olaf quickly try and find a way to stop them, before the party—and all of their hard work—is ruined!

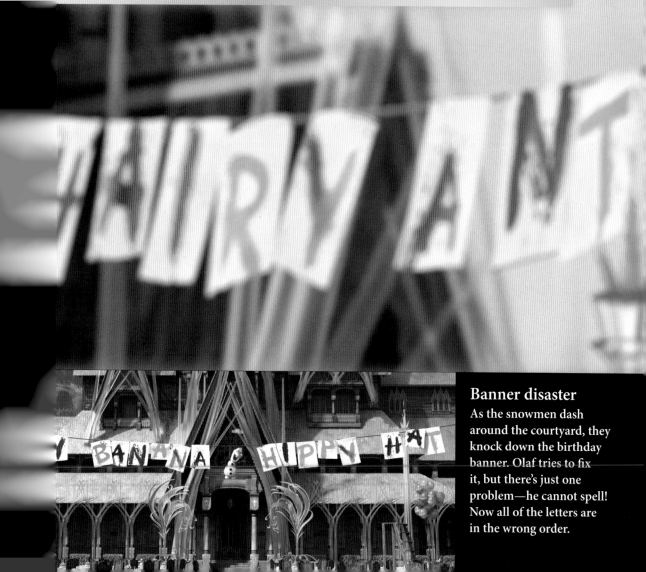

Banner disaster

As the snowmen dash around the courtyard, they knock down the birthday banner. Olaf tries to fix it, but there's just one problem—he cannot spell! Now all of the letters are in the wrong order.

Fighting back

Kristoff comes up with a bright idea to stop the snowmen in their tracks. He stands guard in front of the cake and uses a punchbowl to catch any snowmen who try to reach it.

91

When Kristoff presents Anna with her cake, he accidentally blurts out that he loves her!

PARTY TIME!

When the sisters arrive back at the castle, Kristoff, Sven, and Olaf are still desperately trying to stop the snowmen from ruining the party. However, as Anna opens the gates to the courtyard, Kristoff manages to get everything under control just in time. She is greeted with a wonderful surprise!

BIRTHDAY ANNA

"Best birthday present ever."
Anna

Birthday girl
Anna is truly amazed by her surprise party. As the children of Arendelle lead her into the courtyard, she gazes at her friends in awe. After spending so many birthdays alone in the castle, she finally has people to celebrate with her.

Taking care of Elsa
Elsa wishes she felt well enough to stay at the party, but Anna insists that Elsa needs to get some rest. She tries to make Elsa understand that being able to take care of her sister is the best present she could ever ask for.

Index

DK Penguin Random House

Senior Art Editor Clive Savage
Project Editor Lisa Stock
Editors Lauren Nesworthy, Susan Reuben
Designer Chris Gould
Design Assistants Anna Pond, Amanda Ghobadi
Jacket Designer Lynne Moulding
Senior Pre-production Producer Jennifer Murray
Producer David Appleyard
Managing Editor Sadie Smith
Managing Art Editor Ron Stobbart
Art Director Lisa Lanzarini
Publisher Julie Ferris
Publishing Director Simon Beecroft

First American Edition, 2015
Published in the United States by DK Publishing
345 Hudson Street, New York, New York 10014

Published in Great Britain by Dorling Kindersley Limited.

A catalog record for this book is available from the Library of Congress.
ISBN 978-1-4654-4081-5

DK books are available at special discounts when purchased in bulk for sales
promotions, premiums, fund-raising, or educational use. For details, contact:
DK Publishing Special Markets, 345 Hudson Street, New York, New York 10014
SpecialSales@dk.com

A WORLD OF IDEAS:
SEE ALL THERE IS TO KNOW

www.dk.com
www.disney.com